HIAWATHA
AND
MEGISSOGWON

HIAWATHA
AND
MEGISSOGWON

HENRY
WADSWORTH
LONGFELLOW

ILLUSTRATED BY
JEFFREY THOMPSON

AFTERWORD BY JOSEPH BRUCHAC

NATIONAL GEOGRAPHIC SOCIETY
WASHINGTON, D.C.

On the shores of Gitche Gumee,
Of the shining Big-Sea-Water,
Stood Nokomis, the old woman,
Pointing with her finger westward,
O'er the water pointing westward,
To the purple clouds of sunset.

Fiercely the red sun descending
Burned his way along the heavens,
Set the sky on fire behind him,
As war-parties, when retreating,
Burn the prairies on their war-trail;
And the moon, the Night-sun, eastward,
Suddenly starting from his ambush,
Followed fast those bloody footprints,
Followed in that fiery war-trail,
With its glare upon his features.

And Nokomis, the old woman,
Pointing with her finger westward,
Spake these words to Hiawatha:
"Yonder dwells the great Pearl-Feather,
Megissogwon, the Magician,
Manito of Wealth and Wampum,
Guarded by his fiery serpents,
Guarded by the black pitch-water.
You can see his fiery serpents,
The Kenabeek, the great serpents,
Coiling, playing in the water;
You can see the black pitch-water
Stretching far away beyond them,
To the purple clouds of sunset!

"He it was who slew my father,
By his wicked wiles and cunning,
When he from the moon descended,
When he came on earth to seek me.
He, the mightiest of Magicians,
Sends the fever from the marshes,
Sends the pestilential vapors,
Sends the poisonous exhalations,
Sends the white fog from the fen-lands,
Sends disease and death among us!

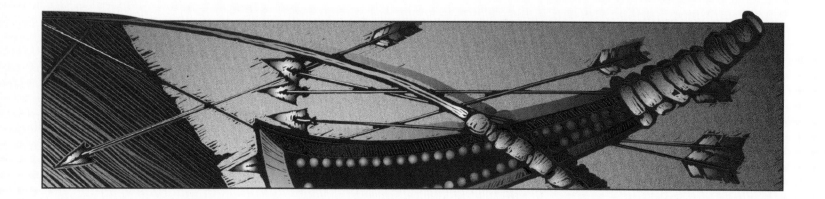

"Take your bow, O Hiawatha,
Take your arrows, jasper-headed,
Take your war-club, Puggawaugun,

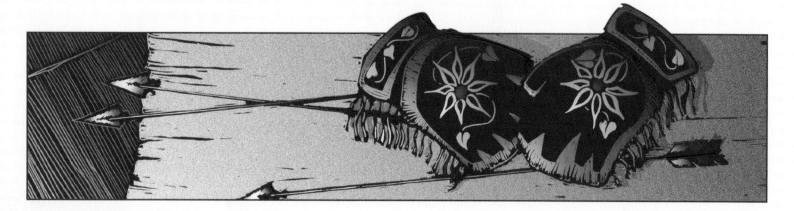

And your mittens, Minjekahwun,
And your birch-canoe for sailing,
And the oil of Mishe-Nahma,

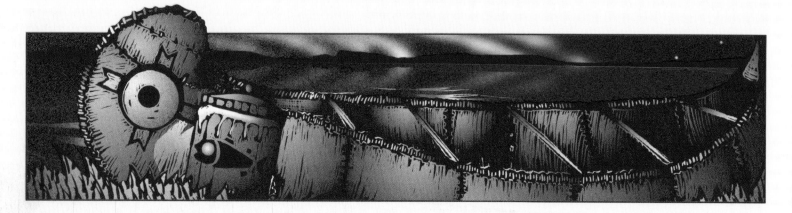

So to smear its sides, that swiftly
You may pass the black pitch-water;
Slay this merciless magician,
Save the people from the fever
That he breathes across the fen-lands,
And avenge my father's murder!"

Straightway then my Hiawatha
Armed himself with all his war-gear,
Launched his birch-canoe for sailing;
With his palm its sides he patted,
Said with glee, "Cheemaun, my darling,
O my Birch-canoe! leap forward,
Where you see the fiery serpents,
Where you see the black pitch-water!"

Forward leaped Cheemaun exulting,
And the noble Hiawatha
Sang his war-song wild and woful,
And above him the war-eagle,
The Keneu, the great war-eagle,
Master of all fowls with feathers,
Screamed and hurtled through the heavens.

Soon he reached the fiery serpents,
The Kenabeek, the great serpents,
Lying huge upon the water,
Sparkling, rippling in the water,
Lying coiled across the passage,
With their blazing crests uplifted,
Breathing fiery fogs and vapors,
So that none could pass beyond them.

But the fearless Hiawatha
Cried aloud, and spake in this wise,
"Let me pass my way, Kenabeek,
Let me go upon my journey!"
And they answered, hissing fiercely,
With their fiery breath made answer:
"Back, go back! O Shaugodaya!
Back to old Nokomis, Faint-heart!"

Then the angry Hiawatha
Raised his mighty bow of ash-tree,
Seized his arrows, jasper-headed,
Shot them fast among the serpents;
Every twanging of the bow-string
Was a war-cry and a death-cry,
Every whizzing of an arrow
Was a death-song of Kenabeek.

Weltering in the bloody water,
Dead lay all the fiery serpents,
And among them Hiawatha
Harmless sailed, and cried exulting:
"Onward, O Cheemaun, my darling!
Onward to the black pitch-water!"

Then he took the oil of Nahma,
And the bows and sides anointed,
Smeared them well with oil, that swiftly
He might pass the black pitch-water.

All night long he sailed upon it,
Sailed upon that sluggish water,
Covered with its mould of ages,
Black with rotting water-rushes,
Stagnant, lifeless, dreary, dismal,
Lighted by the shimmering moonlight,
And by will-o'-the-wisps illumined,
Fires by ghosts of dead men kindled,
In their weary night-encampments.

All the air was white with moonlight,
All the water black with shadow,
And around him the Suggema,
The mosquito, sang his war-song,
And the fire-flies, Wah-wah-taysee,
Waved their torches to mislead him;
And the bull-frog, the Dahinda,
Thrust his head into the moonlight,
Fixed his yellow eyes upon him,
Sobbed and sank beneath the surface;
And the heron, the Shuh-shuh-gah,
Far off on the reedy margin,
Heralded the hero's coming.

Westward thus fared Hiawatha,
Toward the realm of Megissogwon,
Toward the land of the Pearl-Feather,
Till the level moon stared at him
In his face stared pale and haggard,
Till the sun was hot behind him,
Till it burned upon his shoulders,
And before him on the upland
He could see the Shining Wigwam
Of the Manito of Wampum,
Of the mightiest of Magicians.

Then once more Cheemaun he patted,
To his birch-canoe said, "Onward!"
And it stirred in all its fibres,
And with one great bound of triumph
Leaped across the water-lilies,
Leaped through tangled flags and rushes,
And upon the beach beyond them
Dry-shod landed Hiawatha.

Straight he took his bow of ash-tree,
On the sand one end he rested,
With his knee he pressed the middle,
Stretched the faithful bow-string tighter,
Took an arrow, jasperheaded,
Shot it at the Shining Wigwam,

Sent it singing as a herald,
As a bearer of his message,
Of his challenge loud and lofty:
"Come forth from your lodge, Pearl-Feather!
Hiawatha waits your coming!"

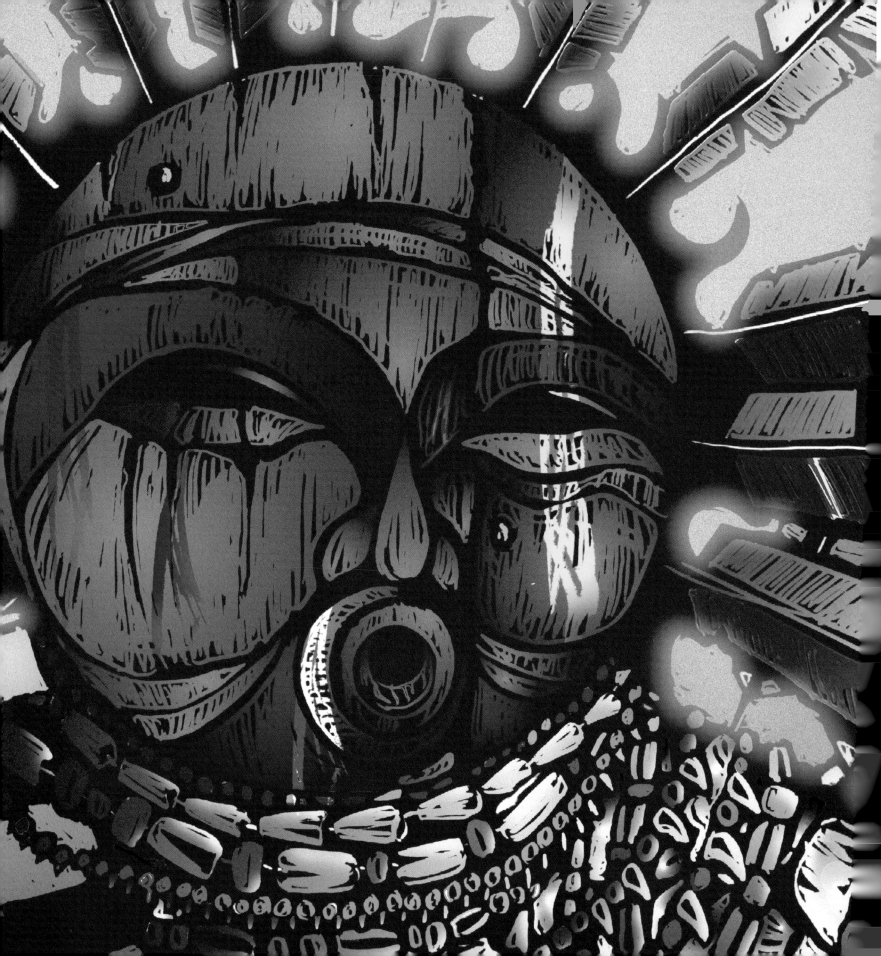

Straightway from the Shining Wigwam
Came the mighty Megissogwon,
Tall of stature, broad of shoulder,
Dark and terrible in aspect,
Clad from head to foot in wampum,
Armed with all his warlike weapons,
Painted like the sky of morning,
Streaked with crimson, blue, and yellow,
Crested with great eagle-feathers,
Streaming upward, streaming outward.

"Well I know you, Hiawatha!"
Cried he in a voice of thunder,
In a tone of loud derision.
"Hasten back, O Shaugodaya!
Hasten back among the women,
Back to old Nokomis, Faint-heart!
I will slay you as you stand there,
As of old I slew her father!"

But my Hiawatha answered,
Nothing daunted, fearing nothing:
"Big words do not smite like war-clubs,
Boastful breath is not a bow-string,
Taunts are not so sharp as arrows,
Deeds are better things than words are,
Actions mightier than boastings!"

Then began the greatest battle
That the sun had ever looked on,
That the war-birds ever witnessed.
All a Summer's day it lasted,
From the sunrise to the sunset;

For the shafts of Hiawatha
Harmless hit the shirt of wampum,
Harmless fell the blows he dealt it
With his mittens, Minjekahwun,

Harmless fell the heavy war-club;
It could dash the rocks asunder,
But it could not break the meshes
Of that magic shirt of wampum.

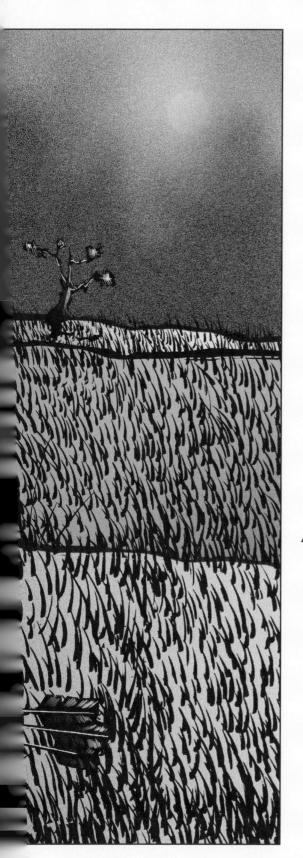

Till at sunset Hiawatha,
Leaning on his bow of ash-tree,
Wounded, weary, and desponding,
With his mighty war-club broken,
With his mittens torn and tattered,
And three useless arrows only,
Paused to rest beneath a pine-tree,
From whose branches trailed the mosses,
And whose trunk was coated over
With the Dead-man's Moccasin-leather,
With the fungus white and yellow.

Suddenly from the boughs above him
Sang the Mama, the woodpecker:
"Aim your arrows, Hiawatha,
At the head of Megissogwon,
Strike the tuft of hair upon it,
At their roots the long black tresses;
There alone can he be wounded!"

Winged with feathers, tipped with jasper,
Swift flew Hiawatha's arrow,
Just as Megissogwon, stooping,
Raised a heavy stone to throw it.
Full upon the crown it struck him,
At the roots of his long tresses,
And he reeled and staggered forward,
Plunging like a wounded bison,
Yes, like Pezhekee, the bison,
When the snow is on the prairie.

Swifter flew the second arrow,
In the pathway of the other,
Piercing deeper than the other,
Wounding sorer than the other;
And the knees of Megissogwon
Shook like windy reeds beneath him,
Bent and trembled like the rushes.

But the third and latest arrow
Swiftest flew, and wounded sorest,
And the mighty Megissogwon
Saw the fiery eyes of Pauguk,
Saw the eyes of Death glare at him,
Heard his voice call in the darkness;
At the feet of Hiawatha
Lifeless lay the great Pearl-Feather,
Lay the mightiest of Magicians.

Then the grateful Hiawatha
Called the Mama, the woodpecker,
From his perch among the branches
Of the melancholy pine-tree,
And, in honor of his service,
Stained with blood the tuft of feathers
On the little head of Mama;
Even to this day he wears it,
Wears the tuft of crimson feathers,
As a symbol of his service.

Then he stripped the shirt of wampum
From the back of Megissogwon,
As a trophy of the battle,
As a signal of his conquest.
On the shore he left the body,
Half on land and half in water,
In the sand his feet were buried,
And his face was in the water.
And above him, wheeled and clamored
The Keneu, the great war-eagle,
Sailing round in narrower circles,
Hovering nearer, nearer, nearer.

From the wigwam Hiawatha
Bore the wealth of Megissogwon,
All his wealth of skins and wampum,
Furs of bison and of beaver,
Furs of sable and of ermine,
Wampum belts and strings and pouches,
Quivers wrought with beads of wampum,
Filled with arrows, silver-headed.

Homeward then he sailed exulting,
Homeward through the black pitch-water,
Homeward through the weltering serpents,
With the trophies of the battle,
With a shout and song of triumph.

On the shore stood old Nokomis,
On the shore stood Chibiabos,
And the very strong man, Kwasind,
Waiting for the hero's coming,
Listening to his songs of triumph.
And the people of the village
Welcomed him with songs and dances,
Made a joyous feast, and shouted:
"Honor be to Hiawatha!"

Is Hiawatha an Authentic Native American Story?

Hiawatha and Megissogwon is most of the "Pearl-Feather" section of Henry Wadsworth Longfellow's book-length epic poem *The Song of Hiawatha,* which was first published in 1853. Longfellow wrote *The Song of Hiawatha* as part of an attempt to create a truly American literature. Though others had written about Native Americans before him, Longfellow was the first non-Native writer to set a work entirely within a Native American cultural context. *Hiawatha* can be seen as the start, a century and a half ago, of literary respect for the oral traditions of Native Americans.

What were the major sources for this American epic? That question is easy to answer. Longfellow turned first to the writings of Henry Rowe Schoolcraft. Schoolcraft traveled as an Indian agent to the Great Lakes area in 1822.

There he married Jane Johnston, the granddaughter of Wabojeeg, a Chippewa chief. (The Chippewa are also known as the Ojibway or the Anishinabe.) Gathering stories with the help of his wife and her family, Schoolcraft recorded the oral traditions of the Chippewa in his first book, *Algic Researches,* published in 1839.

Schoolcraft was one of the first white men to take Native American oral traditions seriously. Before him, it was commonly thought that American Indians were subhuman and had no literature. Longfellow always admitted his debt to Schoolcraft and referred in 1854 in his journal to "Schoolcraft's great book on the Indians." Longfellow based *The Song of Hiawatha* on a series of legends about the great Chippewa trickster Manabozho.

Longfellow was fascinated with Indians all of his life. In 1849 he met Kah-ge-gah-ga-bowh, George Copway, a Chippewa Indian writer and popular lecturer. Longfellow developed a deep respect for Copway's mind and spirit, inviting the Native American author to his home and engaging in long discussions.

But Longfellow's respect for Native American literature doesn't mean that *The Song of Hiawatha* is truly authentic. For one thing, though the source for the plot was Native American, the literary style was from across the sea. Longfellow based the structure of the poetry on the *Kalevala,* the national epic of Finland. He used the trochaic meter of the *Kalevala* so successfully that early critics accused him of plagarism.

And Longfellow made a big mistake. *The Song of Hiawatha* really isn't about Hiawatha at all. The real Hiawatha was a historic figure of great importance, one of the founders of the League of the Iroquois, or Haudenosaunee. How Longfellow chose to give the name Hiawatha to the Anishinabe trickster Manabozho is recorded in a journal entry dated June 28, 1854. Longfellow writes "Work at 'Manabozho,' or, as I think I shall call it, 'Hiawatha,'—that being another name for the same personage." How Longfellow came to be so confused, we don't know.

But *The Song of Hiawatha* is important even if it isn't authentic. A scholar seeking the best source for Aninshinabe stories would not turn to Longfellow, but reading *Hiawatha and Megissogwon* is exciting, even 150 years after its publication, and the popularity of *The Song of Hiawatha* brought our national consciousness one small step towards the appreciation and acceptance of Native American cultures and Native American literature.

JOSEPH BRUCHAC, CONSULTANT

To Oroon Barnes, Susan Abbott and Mary Fredlund…teachers all.
With a nod to Joel Pollack, Patron of the Arts
J.T.

The patterns I used throughout the book were inspired by the traditional craftwork of the Ojibway/Chippewa peoples of the
Northern United States and Canada. The more geometric patterns decorating Megissogwon's clothing are derived from Winnebago designs.

The war clubs, pouches, and the Ojibway canoe were drawn from artifacts on display at the Smithsonian Institution.
The holding hands pattern decorating the borders is derived from a wampum treaty belt I found at the Smithsonian as well.
The horned snake design on Megissogwon's club comes from pictographic etchings cut into rocks near the Great Lakes.
A painting by George Caitlin inspired the handprint on Hiawatha's face.

Special thanks to Joseph Bruchac, who told me where to look, patiently answered all my questions, and helped me pull it all together cohesively.

—Jeffrey Thompson

Illustrations copyright © 2001 Jeffrey Thompson.

To create his artwork, Jef Thompson first drew one element of each illustration, then transferred and cut it into scratchboard (a board covered in a white clay coated with ink). The separate pieces (a figure here, a bird there) were then scanned into a computer and composed in a black and white image of the final illustration. This black and white image was then colored using the computer program Adobe Photoshop. A final image may have as many as ten different elements and, with colors added, may be 80 layers or more in depth.

Text is set in Stone Serif and display text is set in Eaglefeather.
Book design by Bea Jackson, Ivy Pages.
Printed in the United States of America.

Published by the National Geographic Society.

Library of Congress Cataloging-in-Publication Data

Longfellow, Henry Wadsworth, 1807-1882.
[Hiawatha and the Pearl-Feather]
Hiawatha and Megissogwon / by Henry Wadsworth Longfellow ; illustrated by Jeffrey Thompson ; afterword by Joseph Bruchac.
p. cm.
ISBN 0-7922-6676-5
1. Hiawatha, 15th cent.—Juvenile poetry. 2. Iroquois Indians—Kings and rulers—Juvenile poetry.
3. Children's poetry, American. [1. Hiawatha, 15th cent.—Poetry. 2. Iroquois Indians—Poetry. 3. Indians of North America—Poetry.
4. American poetry. 5. Narrative poetry.] I. Thompson, Jeffrey (Jeffrey Allen), 1970- ill. II. Title.
PS2267 .A3 2001
811'. 3—dc21   00-012719

The world's largest nonprofit scientific and educational organization, the National Geographic Society was founded in 1888 "for the increase and diffusion of geographic knowledge." Since then it has supported scientific exploration and spread information to its more than nine million members worldwide. The National Geographic Society educates and inspires millions every day through magazines, books, television programs, videos, maps and atlases, research grants, the National Geographic Bee, teacher workshops, and innovative classroom materials. The Society is supported through membership dues and income from the sale of its educational products. Members receive NATIONAL GEOGRAPHIC magazine—the Society's official journal—discounts on Society products and other benefits. For more information about the National Geographic Society and its educational programs and publications, please call 1-800-NGS-LINE (647-5463) or write to the following address:

National Geographic Society

1145 17th Street N.W.
Washington, D.C. 20036-4688
U.S.A.

Visit the Society's Web site at www.nationalgeographic.com